Burial Machine

BACKLASH
PRESS

A pioneering publishing house dedicated to creating intelligent, vivid books. Established to inform, educate, entertain and provoke.

A Backlash Press Book

First published 2022
Reprinted 2024

Book designer: The Scrutineer, Rachael Adams
Photography: Andrew Vogelpohl

Printed and bound by Ingram Spark

ISBN: 978-0-9955999-2-5

All rights reserved. No part of this publication may be reproduced, stored in a retrieval system or transmitted in any form or by any means, electronic, mechanical, photocopying, recording or otherwise, without permission of the copyright holder.

Copyright © Jacob Griffin Hall
The moral rights of the author have been asserted.

Jacob Griffin Hall

Burial Machine Jacob Griffin Hall

Backlash Poetry

American Dangerous: Renée Olander
The Arsonist's Letters: Michael Tyrell
Bombing the Thinker: Darren C. Demaree
Clay Unbreakables: Natalia I. Andrievskikh
Into The The: Robin Reagler
Phantom Laundry: Michael Tyrell
Tattered Scrolls and Postulates: Joseph V. Milford
The Life in the Sky Comes Down: Bruce Bromley
Unfinished Murder Ballads: Darren C. Demaree

Backlash Journals

#1
#2
#3: Provoke
#4
Isolation
#5

For my friends.

Cover word art by Kelly Caldwell.
Missing you with gratitude and love.

Photography by Andrew Vogelpohl

Burial Machine Jacob Griffin Hall

Contents

What is Beautiful and What Might Be   13

I.

In the End When the World Has Come to Its Final Lurch   17
My Atlanta   19
New Nature   21
I Was Born Small with Something Deliberate in My Name   23
It Was Good to See Him Breathing   25
Echo   27
Where I Learn to Say I Love You   29
Underworld   33
Letter to Family With or Without Reply   35
Signs of Symmetry   37
Again, With Feeling   39
Whistle   41
Trance   43
Event Horizon   45
Declaration   47
My Primary Failure is a Failure of Will   49
The Trouble   51
Offering   53
The Future Tense   55

II.

What if the Wish to Be Precise Survives the World of Objects   59
If You Leave the House Today I'll Be Alone with My Panic   61
Gift   63
Subvocal   73
Washing   75

After a Spring Death We Play Music in the Apartment	77
Planetarium	79
Calling Home	81
Apocalyptica: Spring	83
Apocalyptica: Summer	85
Body Scanning	87
Unconditionalism	89
Myth	91
If I'm Being Honest	93
Alignment	95
Dominion Theory	97
What Once Meant Now Means Differently	99
The Most Critical Component is Movement Itself	101
Alive	103

III.

On the North Shore Trail the Water Touches the Trees	107
Nothing Like It	109
Web Theory	111
Eclogue	113
The Event	115
Interlude	117
Outburst	119
In Order to Establish Perspective	121
Centennial	123
The Neighborhood Has Stenciled the Underpass to Quick Bliss	125
The Neighborhood Has Developed an Appetite for Playful Banter	127
The Neighborhood Has Planted Coneflowers by the Barbed Wire Fence	129
Casting the Watershed	131
At a Bar with You	133
This Outcrop is a Testament	135
To Pasture	137
Melancholy	139
Lily	141
My Animal	143
If Anyone Asks	145
Divinity Gap at Griffey Lake	147
The Universe is Just One of Those Things That Happens from Time to Time	149
Notes and Acknowledgements	151

Burial Machine
Jacob Griffin Hall

Burial Machine Jacob Griffin Hall

> We are dizzy as mercury
> We are solitudes aided by awe
> —Brenda Hillman

Burial Machine Jacob Griffin Hall

What is Beautiful and What Might Be

"Didn't I say we were speaking of autumn
with the remote intensity of a dream?"

Every day I walk
Columbia Cemetery,
past the library,
into the almost-woods
that ache in rainy air
and only sometimes
smell of lavender.
Given the chance, I think
I'd stuff my cruelty
with sweet treats
and make a mockery
of science, dance
beneath a splitting branch
with hands held high,
mythmaking
inside the burial machine.
When I speak
of the future, when I see
the carpenter bee
perched on the edge
of a rotting log,
I don't mean to say
that I don't love you.
Everything I know
is behind me.
Between rows of houses,
I watch mosquitoes
float to their lonely end.
I don't want
to participate in evil anymore.
What else can I say?

Burial Machine Jacob Griffin Hall

I

Burial Machine Jacob Griffin Hall

In the End When the World Has Come to Its Final Lurch

One night when I was a child
I bobbed for apples
and couldn't nip a thing.
When I got home
I devoured a chunk of red
delicious and had skin
stuck in my teeth
for a week. I cried and cried
and refused to play
outdoors. I made friends
with insects and told myself
I would never kill them.
In the end when the world
has come to its final lurch
I'm sure the payoff
will be spectacular. Today
though, is a familiar exercise
in restraint. In 7.5 billion years
the Earth will collapse
into an expanding red giant.
I won't be there to name
whatever it is that's there
and that's probably
beautiful. But for now
a storm rolls in from the east.
The rain hasn't yet
started. On the windowsill
a ladybug tests the air, its red
wings catching the light
at just the right angle
to make it appear unbearable.

Burial Machine Jacob Griffin Hall

My Atlanta

Even now I touch my Atlanta from periphery,
pockets of skyscraper between a mass of old growth,

a snapshot on my laptop background, two days' drive
from home. I watch someone livestream

a family of possums scurrying below a trampoline.
Someone who was not a friend, who once

bought me a beer at a bar off Piedmont, talked comics
before he became violent over the Confederacy.

How much difference did his holstered gun make?
His eyes were beautiful. The light glimmered

on the silver at his hip and I knew that beauty too
could be a weapon. The magnolias are so

glossy green onscreen as the possums dart off
towards the recycling center. By my Atlanta I mean

the life I'm afforded within it. Strawberries
by the river. Arguments in a bar. Sixteen and high,

pulled over in the shadows of an exit
off I-85, told I'm not the kind of guy he's looking for.

Burial Machine Jacob Griffin Hall

New Nature

We gathered by the lake in late November,
the ring of us around the water like a sprocket wheel.
The setting sun gave way to something
repentant, something animal, the two-tone blister
of winter splayed across the dying leaves.
Our bodies gleamed like mechanisms of war,
insular by design, an inheritance. I measured
myself in the distance between my last longing
and my last longing's leavings, initials carved
into the rock face, burnt limbs posed just beneath
a withered strip of oak. There was nothing
beautiful left in the world. Everyone laughed.
The water made objection, nondescript eddies budding
from the plunge of a stone in its heart. I assigned
my body to the landscape encasing it, feared
a loss of magnitude. I imposed my form unduly.
Only the insects took note. We stepped into a world
that wanted its distance, built tombs for those we loved
and marked their graves as our fortunes.
The earth stirred below us as we palmed each hunk
of dirt, placed them in our mouths, celebrated
a cycle of uprooting. I remember the taste of it,
the grubby texture like a fire extinguished on my tongue.

Burial Machine Jacob Griffin Hall

I Was Born Small with Something Deliberate in My Name

When she was three my sister held me
for the first time. A bead of snot hung from her nose.
I blinked and thought I saw my face in a mucus crystal ball
and though we didn't know it, a stranger in the hallway
proclaimed that all was right in the world. For me,
everybody was a stranger. I was tasked with something
impossible: make of the people you meet a permanence.
Permanence was a symbol that still lacked meaning
and though I was two hundred miles away, the waves
still summoned the notion of ocean, of blue.
My sister held me while my mother held a tissue
to her child's nose. The April jays mustered their strength
and attacked the window in coordinated strikes, a baby
in my sister's hands, crying and unaware that the room,
like anything, held its own tiny world, its own idea of breadth.

Burial Machine Jacob Griffin Hall

It Was Good to See Him Breathing

I dreamed his pills
spilled from the plastic bag across the table

and when the wind came at night, my hunger sang like an engine
and the bathtub filled with pollen
and our tattoos were characters hunched in the folds of our skin.

It was good to see him breathing.

Awake I spend my days waiting for the phone call,
waiting at breakfast, waiting in scarcity, waiting with beads
hanging limp from my pocket.

If in the gap between clouds I decipher
our grown stubbornness, maybe he's still waiting alone in Mom's attic
with impatient anger, holding lighter to spoon

as if that combustible could bring the relief of rain.

Burial Machine Jacob Griffin Hall

Echo

Pipes hiss behind the wall
through the new and blue,
morning an ugly cocoon—

ego-white, my polished blush
berates like the scrape of a hangnail.

Burial Machine Jacob Griffin Hall

Where I Learn to Say I Love You

I.

When did I first learn to lock my life away?
I know I saw a stranger walking through an alley

and named the story before its crest.
You twisting wet outside the tattoo parlor,

you beneath the clock tower with a pen against your wrist:
the stranger calling my hands masculine,

a shadow pocket where I learn to say I love you.
I tack a truth to my door in the morning:

me scrubbing naked in front of the mirror,
me holding my scarred stomach in florescent light.

Just like me, I think, to revise my image like soft clay,
to sift my name in wounded private.

Asleep last night I was a boy again
underneath the bleachers, mistaking my lessons in violence

for a path through the world, back strapped
with artificial confidence, chin up, my flowers tucked away

in pockets, unseen and unseeming, colors still
seeking sunlight through dirt-streaked cloth.

I eye the mirror again, edges embroidered
with Queen Anne's lace, trace of purple milkweed.

The morning water washes me, teeth grown thin

Burial Machine Jacob Griffin Hall

with cavities, a prayer contaminating the odds.

I hold my thoughts. You twisting stems again
around stubby knuckles. You sitting on the park bench,

stomach gorged on electricity. I was nine
when I was baptized on a stage as the congregation

held its breath. When I die, I'd like to find a roadside pool,
quiet heat, sparrows circling.

What might it mean to dream a first revision?
I take the nearest hand and make that touch unconditional.

I slide glasses from my face, taste fear and root,
my tongue hung on permission to harm.

Who have I harmed and where do the lessons go
when tenderness sits below a windowsill like an untended flower?

I take a shower and let down my hair.
I try to sing a soft-hearted song. You in the colors

between song and step: you, Jacob,
washing your tongue like slab of concrete under summer rain.

II.

This early summer again. Bagels in a paper bag.
Stranger giving the gift of electric sky: I love you.

Stranger protesting war on the corner of Providence: I love you.
Stranger wading face first into the picket line: I love you.

I find my new permissions and I love you.
I name the weight of an institution and I love you.

I find my way through tall grass to the store and I love you.
My body is scarred and I love you.

My friends sprawled across the middle field and I love you.

My time like a match against the table and I love you.

I love you as the gravel takes new shape.
I love you as magnolia commiserates with wind.

I love you as I learn to learn
the two threads of my imagined life. Between them

I find another life, fingers interlaced like intricate patchwork.
I hold the three in the mirror, my breath against the glass.

I see a boy with dirty hands.
I see a boy in a bathroom hiding from the dark.

I see crying and soap streaks and the sink in living color.
Between two threads of my imagined life I find

a fragility, a pocket with plenty to spare,
[author's name] in a dark bedroom with the bathroom light spilling over.

Burial Machine Jacob Griffin Hall

Underworld

Everything I touch is a replica:
my wrist, little divots in a fruit's rind—

I stand in the kitchen and mind my manners.

Above the sink the ceiling leaks
and I remember my sister's dolls,

remember brushing their hair in the basement,
stowing away to call them my own,

holding them up to the light just to test the idea.

Burial Machine Jacob Griffin Hall

Letter to Family With or Without Reply

To understand
you need to see that uniformity is not a blessing.
You've watched finches share heat on a wire in winter.
You've poured cool water over your child
beneath the sun's summer scorn.
Don't turn from the guilt in your restless bed.
Don't dream an acorn and say miracle.
Every time you take my hand, you extend beyond
the single wish, and in the contours of touch
you brush your heart with dignity.
Forgive me for needing you to reach further.
I am hurting but am far from the only one.
There is another wish at the base of my skull
and there is a world you have abstained from touching.
Growing up, I made maples my markers of future.
You know this. We sat together
and sketched the leaves when no one was looking.
Why, then, are you making alibis
under the light of wildfire? In the dead of night
you nickname the ash oasis.

Burial Machine Jacob Griffin Hall

Signs of Symmetry

Yesterday we walked together in the snow.
It seems self-righteous to describe

the weather
but you're gentle, and I try to be, and when we bicker
insects dot the sky like surgical marks.

Let's start with the text then cross to harder hearts.
Say accountability. Say stigmata. OK,

he's in the hospital again.
Liver not cirrhotic yet. The snapdragon
supposedly

survives well in winter, and in the park M skims her phone
for a diagram comparing addiction
to social acuity.

You grip my hand and squeeze.

It means that sometimes
symmetry is a crisis. Sometimes it lies in wait for you
like a hospital bed

or a florescent bulb grown weak
in the back room.
What's the point of pleasure, you ask, then pick the leather

at the fold of your purse.
I beg justice from the worst of our words.

Say monopoly. Say coolio.
Unsnap the straps on your backpack

Burial Machine Jacob Griffin Hall

and light a lemon scented candle.

If there's something simple, let it be simple.
If there's an ache, then take it for what it's worth.

Again, With Feeling

Who's that in the backyard. Who's playing hopscotch
in the crisp August maw. I will track down my sins
like a hiker tagging constellations in a booklet.
I'll hallucinate safety then waste a week hopping fences
through lazy suburbia. Chestnut stain. Pine straw
rubbing the jean fabric raw. In the hospital lobby
I ate butterscotch candy. It felt entirely unremarkable.

Burial Machine Jacob Griffin Hall

Whistle

Last night I passed out on my neighbor's lawn
because there was a kind of air
that sunk into me, unrequited, as if I had something
to learn from it—something about a blade of grass
and the way it blasphemes rupture,
green and alive, all the shit I'm inclined to put on it.
When I was a child I would sit in the pasture
out back of school, pull a single blade taut
between my thumbs, trouble my mouth against it
like I'd seen other kids do. But no matter
the shape of my lips, no matter the posture
of my small fingers, I couldn't make it whistle,
couldn't loose that sweet pitch like magic
no matter how hard I blew and I knew
that was on me. Sitting alone in that empty field,
not whistling, just not being able to do it—
I thought the blade of grass an appendage,
bold and beautiful. I imagined dying as an imprint
abandoned on the back of someone's lawn.
I pictured god as a mass of hands
sprawled across an empty field, a bit of grass
tucked between the thumbs, unable to make a sound.

Burial Machine Jacob Griffin Hall

Trance

It was Monday night.
I sat in the rain on the sidewalk

stacking pebbles, toeing the border
of the neighbor's yard,

watching monsters skulk behind
a row of parked cars across the street.

It was meatloaf night and I hated it.
I parted my polite lips and watched

moths gather around the streetlight
by the mailbox. I wanted more pebbles.

I wanted my playthings. I wanted
to gather daylilies in a basket.

What if all things took the shape
more or less of their maker?

I scooped my pebbles from the stack
and hurled them into the trees.

Burial Machine Jacob Griffin Hall

Event Horizon

I stand with my family in front of the television.
We watch the screen but really
the screen is an obstacle to sidestep. Really our formation,
shoulder to shoulder like a line of attentive dolls,
is a ruse. We'd all like to say we're just doing our best
but some of us are lying. Some of us watch
the pixels glitch and imagine a planet hanging from a string
on a ceiling mobile. All of us are dizzy,
bloated, staring down the barrel of a future
we'll never quite get the hang of.
Some Tuesday morning years down the road
I'll feel a mosquito nibble my ear and smear it to red oblivion.
If an event horizon by definition
shields its observer from their opposite
then my god, what is light, what is the contrast
between what used to be a mosquito and what persists
as my skin? The future is coming
whether we've got the hang of it or not.
All those years back my mother reaches out
and wipes the television screen free of its gnawing static.

Burial Machine Jacob Griffin Hall

Declaration

July 4th and a pale heat.
Windows all kitsch and cover.

It helps to face the photo of your father
knee-deep in river water.

Green overalls.
Sackful of lures at his hip.

That summer
a Stone Mountain tour:

here's how they churned butter.
Here's Davis and Jackson and Lee beneath the laser lights.

1954: Brown
v Board of Education.

1958: Georgia legislature
approves the purchase of the mountain

at the urging of
a segregationist Governor.

On Providence the construction workers
soak their rags in buckets.

A kid carves a smiley face
into a slab of granite up the street.

The crows are at it again,
in a funk,

Burial Machine Jacob Griffin Hall

as multicolored pinwheels
spin and glimmer.

My Primary Failure is a Failure of Will

I don't believe
the things I know.
In this, I've found
my seams.

In my mouth
a taste of hickory.
In my blood
my doubt. The ritual

burning—
billowed smoke
for the sake
of longleaf pine

or the insatiable
demands
of the Earth, of
the hands

that take land
for their progeny.
All the ground I
walk these Georgia

summers is
fertile. All the ground
takes shape in
that shade of pink

that marks a wound.

Burial Machine Jacob Griffin Hall

The Trouble

I've spent all morning in the pecan grove
sketching salamanders
and sipping coffee from a thermos.
Tonight I'll watch *Poltergeist* on DVD
and lose sleep over the ache
in my left ankle.
Is this familiar to you?
Have you sat on a rusted bucket cracking nuts
beneath a glass bottle?
There's no need to be scared here.
The weeds, too, are orphaned
behind their patch of ugly limestone.
On the side of the barn up the street,
they've made the message clear:
"nothin here worth you dyin over"
which of course means there's no need for killing.

Burial Machine Jacob Griffin Hall

Offering

I distrust the men
talking in the apartment hallway

but I'm lonely here
and the room is thick with stale air
so when the conversation

comes to pause, I whisper through the door
softly to ensure they can't hear me.

In the kitchen I fish vegetables from the sink
and something about that act
makes me think of you, Mom, all those years ago

standing in a pool of drainage overflow
in the hospital parking garage,
assuaging me.

I was surgery-ready and hyperventilating, a ball
of panicked awe, hunched
against the wall below the piping.

You saw me like this
for the first time

as keys dangled from a rubber bracelet
around your wrist, pollen thick on the car's hood.
I was waiting for God

to be good, Mom.
I was stuck in the dank laws of my breath.

I cough into a cloth you gave me for Christmas.

Burial Machine Jacob Griffin Hall

I open the door and offer the men some water.

I distrust the men but even more
I distrust loneliness.

The Future Tense

What a sweet release.
It's uncomfortable to stand in a crowd
being human together.
The moss this time of year
is such a perfect yellow
but the seedlings in the laboratories
hold this story hostage.
Since the goal is either regress
or else hold out a hand
to the future tense,
I'll go on going on without a timer,
with a fistful of dandelion,
ready to make amends
for everything.

Burial Machine Jacob Griffin Hall

II

Burial Machine Jacob Griffin Hall

"What if the Wish to Be Precise Survives the World of Objects"

after Rae Armantrout

The light of a thing
can't account
for why it wobbles
or wilts—

when the doctor
steps into the room
I can't tell
whether she knows

my life or just
suspects
that I've been
going about it wrong.

I think it's
"energy adjacent"
that one end
might be the result

of a formula
while another
just happens to be
what's going on:

unaccountable,
imprecise like
the faux-primrose
by the sink.

Plastic colors

Burial Machine Jacob Griffin Hall

beneath the overhead
florescent, nothing
for us to trim.

If You Leave the House Today I'll Be Alone With My Panic

I can imagine the horses grazing
by the shed in the pasture opposite our house
—the off-limits grounds guarded by a fence
we could easily hop and signs advising us
not to. If you leave the house today
I'll be alone, the other roommates already gone
to work. What if instead of my failing heart
I thought of the neighbor on his porch,
shotgun clutched against his chest?
The best apology is a landscape
full of yellow trees, barbed wire catching sun
above gravel, cattle with backs turned
to the coming rain. If you leave the house today
I'll sit outside and eye the property line,
agonize over the thought: quick trot
through the off-limits, hills thick with flowering,
no one there to call out and stay the gun.

Burial Machine Jacob Griffin Hall

Gift

I credit my panic
to intuition. The blue
vase governs then recedes.
Its sunflowers lie
to my reflection. I suspect
I'll die in this place
but what else
is new.

Burial Machine Jacob Griffin Hall

Burial Machine Jacob Griffin Hall

Burial Machine Jacob Griffin Hall

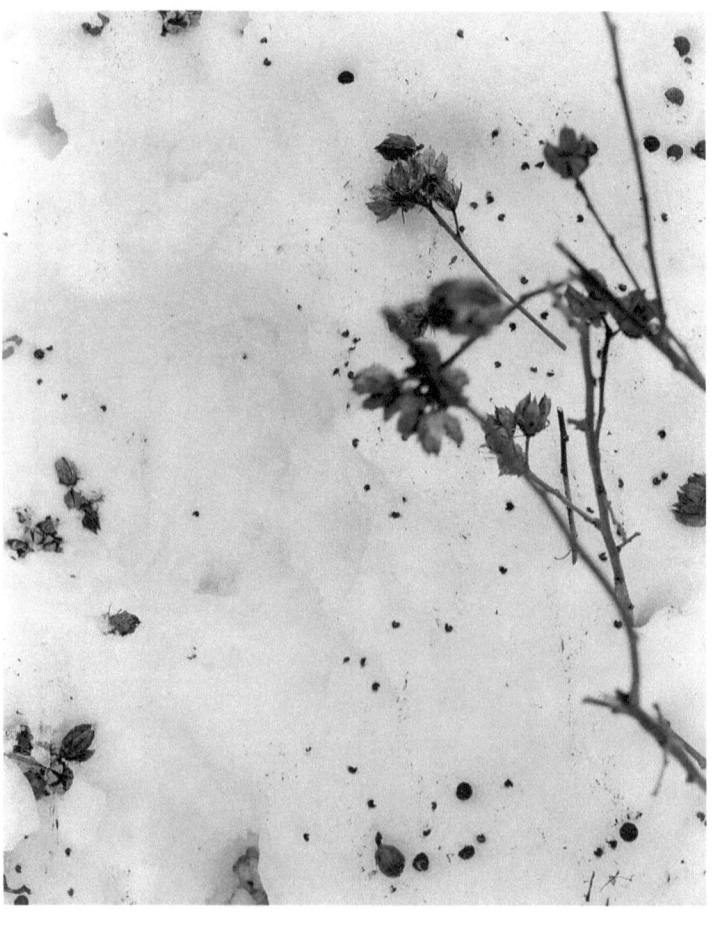

Burial Machine Jacob Griffin Hall

Burial Machine Jacob Griffin Hall

Subvocal

Whether or not there's a name used to give shape to what blooms between people, and whether or not the weather today gives a fair shake to that blooming, the cold wind cold for this region but not for any number of others, the dew still full of color caught in the cradle of its edges, and whether or not you believe there's any use in naming it, you feel it like a stream of too-hot water on the nerves and think this might be the thing that generates order, or pain, or any of the other types of stasis.

Sitting in the café this morning I read and form words discretely in my mouth. I'm embarrassed at the habit. The cashier thumbs through a stack of receipts, yawns beside the pile of cream-colored napkins half-falling over the front of the counter. Imagine, then, the most typical kind of light, sticking to anything it grazes—the kid make-believing a piece of bark outside by the railroad tracks, kicking rocks into the gutter, mother watching across the grass from a park bench, the rich smell of caffè mocha through the whole uncrowded street.

When my friend first told me that she, too, had tried years ago to take her own life, she explained that she didn't mean it, really, in the way she suspected other people meant it. We sat on her front porch. It was raining. I was desperate to find a name for it, the thing blooming between us. I didn't want to doubt her, so I doubted myself, ran my hands over my forehead, through knots in my unwashed hair. I watched a ground beetle scurry along a crack in the stairs, my eyes stuck in the grief it prescribed, frantic legs dodging the rain.

The second train this hour rattles the café windows. I used to play along those tracks, standing on a crosstie during the all clear with my back to the sun: I was Annie Oakley with a pistol at my hip. I was Billy the Kid in *The Left Handed Gun*. Behind the counter the cashier yawns and stands to stretch, browses the internet, glances up at the impeachment. On the other side of the scene, something like a blister swelling with new blood. Annie's hand ready to draw. I watch the titmice sweep over the tracks towards Thrasher

Burial Machine Jacob Griffin Hall

Park, their arc a mark of relief between the trees.

Whether or not we name the thing that blooms between people, my story starts like this: I was at my desk with a handful of pills. I had five roommates and a stack of books and at least one genuine question about cruelty. Now my rule is to err on the side of empathy: on Saturdays I sit in the park and read the news, watch squirrels consort in high branches. I read old books that look to the stars despite the fact that my world is largely starless, having always lived near a city. I practice measured breathing, check my pulse, watch beetles brood in pockets between blades of grass at my feet.

Washing

I wash my cotton smock.
I kick the dirt and clean my shoes.
American robin baring its orange breast.
Neighbors calling the cops.
New medicine atop the cabinet.
New vegetables shipped in from the west.
I press a lost translation.
I take my pills and wash my cotton smock.

Burial Machine Jacob Griffin Hall

After a Spring Death We Play Music in the Apartment

The little
pixie ribbons lean
against a glass
of polished pebbles, storm
outside, your hands still
tapping on the countertop.
You nominate
the tiny pill.
You will the rain to turn machine.
I too enjoy that side of things.
A mellow mix.
The vinyl glitch just skittering
between two beats.
The water chestnuts fill the sink.
We alter basil, name its trim.
Oh holy growing thing.
I'm stuck inside
the absence of.
My fear
is fear of knowing.

Burial Machine Jacob Griffin Hall

Planetarium

Between buildings that choke stem from sky, I find I'm learning my body again. I collect trinkets as birds leave them behind for gather, the peculiar spare parts, their ought that lofts its lack of whole. On the phone this afternoon
      I swore the planetarium windows dozed in the shade of blue I chose for the walls in my childhood bedroom.
That was a lie. There's no planetarium here. It was just something that I imagined.
Early tomorrow morning I'll tell a friend:
      the planetarium. Now that's a thing I'd like to see.

Burial Machine Jacob Griffin Hall

Calling Home

This morning I woke in my life.
In the heart of the first April without irony,

without bees or charred meat tips or honeysuckle strips,
no one watched me, naked beneath the bulb left glowing
from the night before.

No one sat in the corner and thumbed
the abacus beads back and forth.

No one asked for this.
I very well may live
a long and uncontested life.

These are the terms
the script offers.

There's a man
standing outside my window
and I've never been one to wait.

Burial Machine Jacob Griffin Hall

Apocalyptica: Spring

At the edge of "a nothing city"
I cross my legs and watch traffic lights
ride the nothing new.
A man in a blue t-shirt
spills hell through a megaphone
as I thumb the bicycle's spokes below a stairwell.

Burial Machine Jacob Griffin Hall

Apocalyptica: Summer

Earlier today I stood in the market's corner
(husks of corn stacked high by the tomatoes)
and watched an old man
who looked nothing at all like my father
rub a waxy leaf between his fingers
as if *that* were love.

Burial Machine Jacob Griffin Hall

Body Scanning

I measure breath with a ball of yarn.
I have a list of raw materials called my body.

In the morning I fidget with therapy scrawling
and blast *sorry sorry* through the bedroom walls.

Weren't you saying something about bad dreams
and weren't we pretending to sleep again?

Say *sorry sorry* then begin to scan: feet heavy
on carpet; ache in my left calf; last breath stuck

between chest and upper abdomen.

Burial Machine Jacob Griffin Hall

Unconditionalism

No matter how far I've come
to meet my place among the living, and no matter how far
I'll go with a word hitched to the back of my tongue
(the word mundane—maybe burial
or cauliflower or machine), and no matter how many times
I've marked myself *a self*, skin posed in white light
as rain begins to fall over a farmhouse,
or mantle of marble all my own, or doe writhing in pain on the interstate
at night, a gash catching headlights between two front limbs,
and no matter what this wakes in me, no matter the shame
I'm unable to pin down, no matter the squirm in my gut that won't slip
into the world, into the past's pastures, no matter
how I twist my body, how I contort at night as I undress alone
in bed, my skin hot, my *one* under attack, and no matter how
that heat treats me, and no matter
how I treat my own people, which should be but is not all people,
and no matter the lights flickering beneath the doorframe,
and no matter my conviction, and no matter the earth swollen
in my neighbor's yard, another animal grazing in the garden,
a taste in my mouth that just won't fade.

Burial Machine Jacob Griffin Hall

Myth

Once the earth's
husk hung its back
to the passing black
and solidified,
waited for
a punchline,
a hot little ball of light.
Despite this
I'm sick of mining
my past lives for clues.
From now on
I'll enjoy looking
at the flowers
and refuse
to pick them.
When comedy
is a dead language
and the weeds
have all flown off
to the moon,
I'll make my peace
with breakfast, science,
the little balloon
tied to my blue mailbox.

Burial Machine Jacob Griffin Hall

If I'm Being Honest

On my worst days I take stock of the ways
the world seems to narrow. I spread tarot cards
and bits of vegetables on my kitchen counter.
I tend the flower in the window like my life depends
on its blossom, like rain spilling from gutters
could be a measure of breath, my lungs expanding,
the room a swollen bulge of air. If when I die
heaven is just a chemical reaction in my brain, I think
I'd be fine with that. I do my best not to care
for the pang of nostalgia. If there are no sparrows
painted on my urn, I hope someone reads
the empty space as a kind of kindness. The universe
is expanding and with it go my body, the pine trees,
the jackfruit stacked high at the international market.

Burial Machine Jacob Griffin Hall

Alignment

Caught up in the way the gravel
replicates distraction, green stem
kneaded to mud. Churchill's Grocery,
nine a.m., throated cough
on a buggy's little lascivious wobble.
Today there is no backdrop.
No moat moaning its lesser branches.
I pocket my list of casual dead
and go on shopping, leafy greens,
pile of plums on my last pass through,
the aisle "mist and mist-grey, no colour."

Burial Machine Jacob Griffin Hall

Dominion Theory

If value comes
not from a thing

but from the way
a thing inhabits

space, and if light
is just another type

of lesser evil,
maybe the most

justifiable way to live
is to cede life

and also power
if it comes to you.

Below a flickering
bulb, I stand in

shame, shout down
intrusive thoughts

while asparagus
cooks in the oven.

Burial Machine Jacob Griffin Hall

What Once Meant Now Means Differently

One by one the stars
have been obliterated. I touch the gaps
between my teeth. I can't believe how impractical I've been,
       tinkering with smoke detectors, checking the time
for flaws. Listening to my friends laugh, planets caught
like clumsy orbs in their mouths, I doubt my conviction
            that they occasionally love me.
This whole morning is a skein of yarn
unspooling. I watch it spiral from its beautiful
dirty knots.

Burial Machine Jacob Griffin Hall

"The Most Critical Component is Movement Itself"

after George Rickey's sculpture "Column of Four Squares"

With the wind at my back, I can't imagine
that anything lacks
        the capacity for patience. Yesterday for example
            in the afternoon smear

the boiler coil set a drop of water to steam—
        my body aligned
with every other orbit in the room. It was the movement
we'd all been waiting for. Light dripped through

the blinds, a matter of raw kinetics. The coil
                          grew deadly red.

For a moment I forgot my posture altogether
        and set my fingers drumming

over the washcloth's threads. Within each tension
an artifact.   I listened to the planet's slow grind,
the sun widening, the blacks of my eyes
        in pivot.

Burial Machine Jacob Griffin Hall

Alive

after Joy Harjo

There's enough tension riding the beetle's gasoline wings
to fill a chest with heat, rapid beating—
there's enough light coating the polyester curtains
to convince me   that faith
                                  is a lonely condition,
a whimper in the mouth, steady then not
        a thing at all.
I take it all like gospel. I hold my soggy tongue
in my hands. It is what I have
to give you.

Burial Machine Jacob Griffin Hall

III

Burial Machine Jacob Griffin Hall

On the North Shore Trail the Water Touches the Trees

I will sit in this moment and remember what is ordinary.
I will share this with my lover and drink pomegranate tea.

We will take a walk around the lake.

Not a single cloud in the sky.
Today I'm stranded in my body under a cloudless sky.

On the wet rock where bullfrogs celebrate their theories of spring
I will find a tube of lipstick and bask alongside them.

There is no theory of being in the world
that is not also a theory of the world.

We will brush our hair and look beautiful.

Burial Machine Jacob Griffin Hall

Nothing Like It

If home is a challenge
I'll take some time to erase the quiet of things.

I'll ease my luck into the issue
and livestream Plath hanging from her window scattering birdseed.

O chilly autumn evenings.
O condition transforming the microbiome.

Home is a challenge and that's what I can stomach for now.

When I was a boy I held my hands to the sky
and pleaded God, no, God.

When I bathed I picked my feet to catastrophe.

O chilly autumn evenings.
O product blogger dancing offscreen.

Human love is a small part of paradise.
I drink in the angry day.

Burial Machine Jacob Griffin Hall

Web Theory

The watershed spreads like a web of belief. I tape my wrong
to a string of *what ifs—what could be* stills mud-stuck in the rift.
The streams drift like two slivers of the same split tongue.
I browse the internet and make news of the common, hurl stones
into water, watch damselflies scatter from their feeding.
I glance down at the screen: "An ecological network is a representation…"
"A silken structure created by the animal…" I follow the thread
from algae to tadpole, hyla chrysoscelis, hyperlinked Cooper's hawk
gnawing its catch between needles at the peak of an eastern white pine.
I blink and scroll, dip my toes into the water below the rockface,
bellow from my gut, trees bent above the pollywog's wavelet
like a labor of love in the swarm. This link isn't a solution.
All I know is something is bound to break. All I feel today is fragile.
I slide my phone into my pocket, toss a final rock,
the ripple a map of my world.

Burial Machine Jacob Griffin Hall

Eclogue

"To say it is mindless is missing the point"

We head down to the chapel pond
where cinnamon ferns arc their fronds over water.

The landfill fire still burns five months on
but the fire is in the city, two hours south,

and the long rows of houses with soot-stained windows
are not particular to us: the apples and oats and particulate dust

of Fulton County are not the pond, not the fronds
brushing ankles, not the minerals or bust of rock we trust

to hold us in place. What does the water say about ash
on a southern gust? I find an ethics on the bluff:

the contours of what leans against. The touch that bares tension,
water on leaf, smoke snug in the crease of asthmatic lungs,

in the divots of a songbird nest. Whose justice is this?
By the pond I cross-stitch a green thread into white backdrop.

Burial Machine Jacob Griffin Hall

The Event

If beneath a branch some unknown animal
has gnawed a leaf, and if by chance a person sees

the leaf on an afternoon walk through the arboretum,
bends down to scoop the leaf and take it along,

makes no big thing of it, just kneels on the sidewalk
for the leaf, for the leaf but also for the gnawing,

if the person kneels then stands, deposits the leaf
in a pocket, there will be a fact in the leaf and a fact

in the pocket, each turning over the other's quiet claim.

Burial Machine Jacob Griffin Hall

Interlude

The river behind my apartment is lazy gray
and full of plastic. No one fishes there,

not the kids who grew up fishing,
not the parents who climb Sunday stairs.

On clear days, waterfowl come
to those who tend chickens, those people

who take thick bites of apples, keep the chickens
close to their hearts. Nightjars land

on porches, watch the bodies
pray in the dark. Sometimes a deer emerges

by the river, dips into the water, parched.

*

My dresser drawer collects its wings:

little evil, little dopamine. I feel it rattling
in the far corner of the room.

I pocket the busheled maroon
stolen from my neighbor's yard, insular mark,

my blinds picked apart at the edges.
I strike matches, slam latches on the door.

Oath-maker, sun-taker, barrel full
of burning leaves.

Burial Machine Jacob Griffin Hall

Lion's-eye, devil-sky, Sunday best
with bended knees.

Outburst

Dougherty Bridge hangs behind the tracks
like a still life lacking magic.
A mother covers her child's bare feet
beside the polluted creek, a cast
around her wrist, simple robin's nest
tucked in a gap in the overpass.

There's no dignity in paraphrase.
There's a broken rake and five men
in masks by the stadium.
There's a trapdoor in the manor across town
that drops down to a crisis bunker
stocked with rifles and rations.

I hear the street talker's last sermon.
I bury my face in my hands screaming fire, fire, fire.

Burial Machine Jacob Griffin Hall

In Order to Establish Perspective

In the old paradigm
I flung my body
like a skipping stone
against each ridge
in the Chattahoochee's
wide mouth.
I worshipped insects
and held landscape
accountable for the grief.
As if in a trance
I ate boiled peanuts
and watched flocks
brush against treetops
as the dam released
to high sirens.
I came across a friend
sitting on the bank,
wet sand caked
to his ankles, a needle
in his arm.
The river fowl craned
their wiry necks
then shoved off
in one coordinated gasp
towards a pyre
burning over the pinewood.

Burial Machine Jacob Griffin Hall

Centennial

In the river park the old music
stakes its claim to your new kind of listening.
Everywhere the grasshoppers
are in tantrum. First, something is novel
then all of a sudden the world has realigned.
Sometimes you don't see it coming.
Sometimes you just want that lonely star
to mind its own business. The music plays
and there are streamers littering
the low branches over the water, tadpoles
stuck in a spit-thick patch of mud.
You can smell the hickory, which matters
more than it should to you. A woman
closes her eyes and runs her wet fingers
over her face. Another thumbs the lace cloth
draped over the table. It seems like eternity
is an impractical thing to participate in.

Burial Machine Jacob Griffin Hall

The Neighborhood Has Stenciled the Underpass to Quick Bliss

God, what a pleasure.
God bless chamomile tea and Miles Davis
running the voodoo down from the neighbor's porch.
What apart from this can amount to anything today?
God bless peaches under the bridge, every heart
stuck on the hummingbird's speed between windchime
and red flower. Afternoon hours. Friendly zucchini bread
in a paper sack. The gaps between houses and gaps
between trees and gaps between trumpet blasts
as sirens pass behind Peachtree Street.
This heat is premature. Under the gutters the flowers
make every house a spectacle.

Burial Machine Jacob Griffin Hall

The Neighborhood Has Developed an Appetite for Playful Banter

If you want to talk ghosts we'll talk ghosts.
We've got a knack for this charismatic
back and forth underneath the makeshift veranda.
Make it candid. Take a friend and flop ass-first into the puddles
by the chain link fence. Call out to the Dowdy house
making art from cardboard scrap, crafting black bracelets
from plundered rubber. The neighborhood has an evil eye
and buttermilk biscuits, just the right amount of manners.
If you want to talk nails we'll talk hammers.
If you want a spectacle we'll turn the backyard into a festival:
look at the ochre flowerpots. The whole garden
spins its above-ground bloom.

Burial Machine Jacob Griffin Hall

The Neighborhood Has Planted Coneflowers by the Barbed Wire Fence

Better stagnant than sadness.
Better new buds than blood on the wire.
Around here, we'll yell over the sound of the blow dryer,
eat chips and ease our hips into street music.
Count syllables. Denounce universals. Seven-layer dip
on the lips of drag queens and music fiends
and sips of skunk beer from the neighbor's styrofoam cooler.
Better lovebirds than battle scars.
Grab a gas station cruller and a cup of hot coffee.
Watch the stems lean against the chain-link, city lights
between slats of ecstatic trees, nothing more
comfortable, the whole block singing.

Burial Machine Jacob Griffin Hall

Casting the Watershed

For now, I'll do away with what lack
I hold in funny spaces,
catch the turmoil of reeds in a powder keg.
I've set my sin aside, so what more
does the migratory heat hold in prayer?
And what about that alternate world
where flowers grow on the same stalks
and I talk for hours in the library
with some strangeness? What about all that
call and repose that goes unheeded
in this world, where flowers dangle
like stirrups, little pewter pumps of grief?
I say, for now, and while we can,
let's take my life's many floras and hold them
in a basket, pass them around for any
who might discern their petals combustive.

Burial Machine Jacob Griffin Hall

At a Bar with You

When the wet stem stuck to your finger
and the cherries floated in the jar

the room vanished and the red syrup vanished
but the sun through the blinds brought to eye

our combined anatomy, a would-be brush
with creation. Now I count the scars on my body.

You watch foam spill from the edge
of your cup. We're here together, finding ways

to levitate. The plums are on the countertop
and nothing could be more respectable than that.

If the world came to exist in a single moment,
I'm sure it smelled like this—two bodies

laughing and sweating, making sense then not.
I'm finding new ways to imagine our life

and you're finding wet soil in a flowerpot.
There are moments that open and wait for you.

There's a light in the room
that resembles the passing of time.

Burial Machine Jacob Griffin Hall

This Outcrop is a Testament

I wrap my hands around a bundle of vines
dangling beside the magnolia. The sun slits a sour petal

and opens *the seam of things*. I can almost see it—
white stitch in the Chattanooga sky.

I try to name the puncture of the tomato lattice,
divide bulb from stem as shade takes hold of the garden.

I take a tonic from a stranger and tuck it in my pocket.
Regarding the pain of others, I'm often

at a loss. My own worlds are lessening. I'm no healer.
In the dome head of the willow a caterpillar straps in

for a ride. Sunlight derides my inaction, a reciprocity tree.

Burial Machine Jacob Griffin Hall

To Pasture

The sky is desperate for an anchor
to tie around its ankles, like that weight
could be an aphorism that would hold
everything in place. The afternoon

cuts across the rhubarb in the garden,
quick through the far fields of cotton
stretched against the trees. The children
are laughing and they are nowhere

to be found. A leaf falls from the gutter
over the basset hound as it lumbers up
the stairs onto the front porch. Two
blocks over the street is handcuffed

to an unpaved spurt of grass, its wrist
a mast of true need witnessed without
concern in this vast stretch of Colquitt
County, water pooled in its chest

like spring runoff. The sun is bleeding
again and no one knows how to save it
as the supper bell rings clattering across
the driveway, out through the row crop

until it reaches a labored ear and dissipates.

Burial Machine Jacob Griffin Hall

Melancholy

It's not that I can't imagine another world.
If that makes me sad so be it.

The baby's breath sits
in a panel of multiple frames:
a face that evades hell, scrapes thistle,

a lemon's acidic spiral
that marks it vulnerable, therefore true—
in each of the many worlds

I stand in a crowd and watch the lemon plunge.

Burial Machine Jacob Griffin Hall

Lily

Months ago you told me a joke. I contorted my body, experimented with angels. *How you interpret the joke* you said *depends on whose world you live in*. Between the leaves the sun was casual with its subatomic particles in collision. *Is the joke tragic?* That wasn't my question to ask. The petals fit the backdropped sky like a children's mask. Water dripped from the neighbor's spigot as the planet held tight to its pocket of time. You told me the joke and the next day I saw tiger lilies everywhere. I wasn't sure if I had just begun to notice them or if there had been some massive overnight planting. Little almost-black spots against orange bloom. Sunburst. *A real, primal heat.* That night I buried myself in the computer screen and read about spring flowers. I read about the rising sun and then the Manhattan Project. Lise Meitner wasn't awarded the Nobel Prize for her work on nuclear fission. Later she abhorred the creation of the bomb and refused to participate. Maybe she heard the news on the radio one day and closed her eyes. Whose world do I live in? Who interprets the meaning?

Burial Machine Jacob Griffin Hall

My Animal

These new summers
sit on the skin
like an ill-fitted garment.

The Erie shoreline
whips high

catches glare
from traffic lights at each
end of the suspension

bridge. Mayflies swarm
the buildings'
brick sides and tonight

they will die
in heaps.

The perch will continue
to feed on their bodies

the whole animal mass
a state of
becoming. With all

this happening,
each instance insisting
on the same

long story, how can I stand
to see it
with a deep skull?

Burial Machine Jacob Griffin Hall

At my best I'll try to forget
my embedded edges

let the objects
take me

me my animal
into their measure of what
can be tethered

try to let the sound
be and not be
isolated, a raw mouth

a particle drawn to light.

If Anyone Asks

Two days of rain collects in a pool by the mailbox.
In another life I sat by a fire and stitched jewels into my sleeve.

I breathe in this other life, fog on my glasses,
the pool gathering species below me. On a day just like this,

two Mays and a botched attempt at faith
into the future, I'll reconsider the water's collapse

below a spring leaf, the tree's photosynthesis,
the asteroids spinning from their chains.

For now, my game is an image.
The politicians spit into their dirty mugs.

Water striders skim the surface, making ripples, making mazes,
making a peculiar kind of love. If anyone asks,

this is my axis—I'm through standing over the puddle
and I'm through needing to decipher it.

Burial Machine Jacob Griffin Hall

Divinity Gap at Griffey Lake

A woodpecker names the day
a shade of bright persistence
The year lengthens then constricts

The bird's body sits
splitting the gap between leaves like an atom,
yawning, slick dew adorning the bill—

lakeside I take a knife and run
the blade against a table's oblong edge
Of course it gives

The blade and the bird exchange their visions
finding heat in the capacity to middle.

Burial Machine Jacob Griffin Hall

The Universe is Just One of Those Things That Happens from Time to Time

I deposit my tired universe of bones
beside the farmhouse. Discrete, the butterfly weed
with its leaves tapered to a soft point
leans against the lower stem of a coneflower.
I eat sweet bread and strawberries
and stare into the pocket of oaks dawdling
at the far edge of the field. I draw rings in the clouds
with my outstretched finger, the posture
not unlike accusation, the hair erect at the brush
of a spider against an exposed ankle. The only choice
is how far to carry a burden. I've known
the most ordinary people, autumn, untamed piles
of burning leaves. I've watched from a safe distance
and disregarded the intensity with which I scratched
my wrist, the skin slick and glinting
beneath a series of similar suns. I've negotiated
my right to fathom the bodies of insects.
It's going well so far. I've given up
chocolate bars and late nights and thoughts
of making my life a metaphor. Still the coneflower
is nimble atop its spread of fibrous root.
I wait for the sun to stain the clouds
that shade of rattled yellow that announces evening,
the low light, a thing I know but still need to parse.

Burial Machine Jacob Griffin Hall

Notes and Acknowledgements:

The epigraph for the book is from Brenda Hillman's poem "Phone Booth," from her collection *Practical Water*

The epigraph for "What Is Beautiful and What Might Be" is from Mary Ruefle's poem "Glory," from her collection *Cold Pluto*

"Signs of Symmetry" is a title taken from Dana Swimmer's album *Veloce*. They are no longer a band, but you can still listen on Spotify

The epigraph for "Event Horizon" is from the Wikipedia page of the same name

"What if the Wish to Be Precise Survives the World of Objects" is a phrase from Rae Armantrout's poem "Hell," from her collection *Wobble*

In "Alignment," the phrase "mist and mist-grey, no colour" is from H.D.'s *Trilogy*

"The Most Critical Component is Movement Itself" is a quote from the sculptor George Rickey about his kinetic art

In "Web Theory," "An ecological network is a representation…" and "A silken structure created by the animal…" are taken from the Wikipedia pages for "Ecological Network" and "Spider Web," respectively

The epigraph for "Eclogue" is from Camille T. Dungy's poem

"Characteristics of Life," from her collection *Trophic Cascade*

"The Universe is Just One of Those Things That Happens from Time to Time" is a quote from an NPR radio special on cosmology and astrophysics

Thank you to the following journals and their editors for publishing versions of these poems and supporting my work. I am endlessly grateful:

Communion Arts Journal – "Eclogue"

DIAGRAM – "What if the Wish to Be Precise Survives the World of Objects"

Figure 1 – "Interlude" and "Outburst"

Ghost City Review – "Signs of Symmetry"

The Indianapolis Review – "Event Horizon"

LandLocked – "Alive" and "Centennial"

Menacing Hedge – "To Pasture"

New Ohio Review Online – "The Universe is Just One of Those Things That Happens from Time to Time"

New Orleans Review – "If You Leave the House Today I'll Be Alone With My Panic"

New South – "Casting the Watershed" and "New Nature"

semicolon – "What Once Meant Now Means Differently"

Split Rock Review – "Whistle"

Andrew Vogelpohl

I am a black and white photographer from Williston, Ohio. Photography has opened me to a world where darkness helps to develop character. Chicago, Illinois is my current home and aside from photography, I enjoy vinyl records, cooking, and evading routine with my cat Ramona.

Burial Machine Jacob Griffin Hall

www.ingramcontent.com/pod-product-compliance
Lightning Source LLC
LaVergne TN
LVHW041638060526
838200LV00040B/1615